POVERTY

I0502634

IS

NOT

YOUR

FRIEND

ACKNOWLEDGEMENT

I WOULD LIKE TO SINCERELY THANK MY LORD
AND SAVIOR JESUS CHRIST. I ALSO THANK MY
WIFE, ELIZABETH, AND MY FOUR BEAUTIFUL
CHILDREN:
AELISHA, CHRISTOPHER, SAIGE M'REE AND TIFFANY
JUST FOR BEING ALIVE AND IN MY LIFE.

POVERTY IS NOT YOUR FRIEND

CAUSES OF POVERTY ACCORDING TO PROVERBS

BY

Craig "WYZEMAN" Cade

Table of Contents

INTRODUCTION 4

RICH HAND, POOR HAND 5

CONSTRUCTION VS. DESTRUCTION 7

STOP BEING STINGY 9

RICHES CAN'T BE TRUSTED 11

TROUBLING YOUR HOUSE 13

LAZY BONES 15

SLUG LIFE 17

WHERE'D YA GET THOSE RICHES? 19

VAIN MONEY 21

CAN'T TELL ME NUTHIN' 23

GIVE ME MY INHERITANCE AND YOURS, TOO 25

QUIT BELLY ACHIN' 27

I HEAR YA TALKIN' BUT 29

AN IDLE SOUL 31

HURRY, HURRY! 33

YOU SNOOZE, YOU LOSE 35

P.O.W.E.R. 37

EDWARD LAZY HANDS 39

REVERSE ROBIN HOOD 41

COSIGN BLUES 43

EAT, DRINK, SLEEP, AND BE BROKE 45

FROM THE GREEDY TO THE NEEDY 47

LEAD NOT INTO TEMPTATION 49

SIN: THE BLESSING BLOCKER 51

DISCIPLES OF VANITY 53

HASTE NOT, WANT NOT 55

THE EYES OF POVERTY 57

POOR? WHAT POOR? 59

LOOSE WOMEN, LOST MONEY 61

VISION: CHERISH OR PERISH 63

INTRODUCTION

Let's face it. Poverty is not our friend. It is not a toy. It is not a playmate. It is not a figment of our imagination. It is a vile spirit on special assignment to kill, steal and destroy: **I am come that they might have life, and that they might have it more abundantly** (John 10:10).

The spirit of poverty has an assignment to block the abundant life that God has given us through Christ, by any means necessary. Poverty attacks our wealth, health, well-being, and anything else that represents the goodness of God. We have already been given this wonderful gift of abundant life through Jesus. We have been given **the Blessing of the LORD that makes rich and adds no sorrow (Proverbs 10:22).**

We must understand that an elaborate deception has been formed to keep us from receiving what God has so graciously given. It comes in various forms; many of which will be discussed in this writing. No matter the form, anything that comes to inhibit the Blessing of the LORD from getting to your life all stems from the spirit of poverty.

A popular mantra has infiltrated the body that we are to pursue riches. Contrary to this ideology, that belief is unscriptural. *Why would we have to go get a blessing that has already been given?*

In Deuteronomy 28:2, Moses tells God's people: **And all these blessings shall *come on thee*, and will *overtake thee*, if thou shalt hearken unto the voice of the Lord thy God.** In the New Testament, Jesus tells us in Matthew 6:33: **But seek ye first the Kingdom of God and His righteousness and all these things shall be *added* unto you.**

The truth is that poverty seeks to *take from* you what God wants to get *to* you. The Word comforts us saying, **"Fear not, little flock; for it is your Father's good pleasure *to give you* the kingdom** (Luke 12:32 emphasis mine). Make no mistake: God wants us blessed. God wants us prosperous. God is glorified when we are blessed.

For I know the plans I have for you," declares the LORD, "plans to prosper you and not to harm you, plans to give you hope and a future." (Jeremiah 29:11 NIV)

yThough this truth is verified throughout the Bible, it still is highly controversial. However, my purpose in this writing is not to debate this issue, but to expose the enemy causing this controversy – poverty. I have also chosen to limit my search to the book of Proverbs which is chock full of poverty's antics and destructive practices. Remember this. We don't haves to strive to get something that is already ours. Prosperity is ours through Christ. Poverty does not want us to know that and has put up smoke screens and road blocks to keep prosperity from flowing to us. We don't take showers to add clean *to* our bodies, but rather to remove the dirt *from* them. My mission is to show the devastating effects of poverty and how to eradicate them from our lives. Only when poverty is moved out can prosperity move in. Join me in this quest and let us all be blessed together. Amen!

RICH HAND, POOR HAND

HE BECOMETH POOR THAT DEALETH *WITH* A SLACK HAND: BUT THE HAND OF
THE DILIGENT MAKETH RICH.

Proverbs 10:4

He becomes poor that deals with a slack hand;

But diligent hands make a rich man.

A minister friend of mine once told me of a story of the mysterious "money hand." In certain parts of Southern Louisiana, a person could pay a woman five hundred dollars to "bless" their hands so that they could easily attract money. He told of how a few of his friends had visited this woman and the result was far from a blessing. They were ecstatic to find themselves winning gambling bets, poker games, card games and the like, but their success was to be short lived. Nearly every one of them died a mysteriously tragic death. One friend was found dead in the front seat of his car with a briefcase filled with over $250,000 laid across his chest.

This, dear reader, is not God's idea of hands that make one rich. One might ask, "what kind of hands *do* make one rich and how can I get a pair?" Well, before we tackle that, we must first determine what makes a person's hands poor. After all, this book is meant to expose poverty and its causes. The Hebrew meaning for "slack," according to Strong's Exhaustive Concordance is deceitful, treacherous, or slothful. Consequently, the Hebrew meaning for "hand" in this context is figuratively: power. If we were to put together a rough English translation of this, then it might read: He becomes poor that deals in *power* that is *deceitful, treacherous or laz*y. Any such power or "hand" is not from God and therefore can only bring poverty in the end.

What about the elephant in the room? The rich, many of which do not profess that God even exists; much less that He is the Source for their riches. In fact, many rich in this world deem themselves as "self-made millionaires." However, the truth is that that mentality is still a poor man's mentality, because it emanates from a "slack" power source. It is derived from *will* power and not *real* power. Poor deals can only lead to poor results.

Conversely, the Hebrew word for diligent is a mining term related to a dug trench or mined gold. It is much more than hard work or effort. It is wise, incisive, ever-improving work. It is not just practice making perfect, but *perfect* practice making perfect. It is wise, perfect work, therefore a "diligent hand" can be labeled as perfect power. That kind of power can only come from the perfect Source – God.

Hands that are slack are hands that bring lack.

What Hand Are You Dealing Life?

CONSTRUCTION VS. DESTRUCTION

THE RICH MAN'S WEALTH *IS* HIS STRONG CITY:

THE DESTRUCTION OF THE POOR IS THEIR POVERTY.

Proverbs 10:15

A man's strong city and his wealth are the same

And a poor man is destroyed by poverty's shame.

The literal translation of the beginning of this passage regarding the rich says that "wealth is the city of his strength" To the rich, their riches are their dwelling place. Wealth is the not only the foundation but the very construct of their method of operation. The wealthy (at times to their hurt) make decisions based on the strength of their city. The word "strong" in this verse means *might* or *boldness*. Their choices in life are made boldly. As to where they eat, what they drive, what they wear and where they live, wealth is usually the impetus for these decisions. This is not inherently bad, but unfortunately such privilege brings temptation toward greed, arrogance and pride. God's intention for riches was not to produce these negative characteristics for Proverbs 10:22 says: *The blessing of the LORD maketh rich and He addeth no sorrow with it.* God blessed Abraham richly. Abraham is regarded as the "father of faith" and that faith was in God and not his riches. Scripture says that *"Abraham was very rich in cattle, in silver, and in gold"* (Genesis 13:2). Abraham, though he was very rich, did not regard these riches as his city. As a matter of fact, Hebrews 11:10 tells us that *"he looked for a city which hath foundations, whose builder and maker is God."* We can see then that wealth is a gift of God but is never to be a substitute for Him.

So, if God approves of wealth when used appropriately, then does He disapprove of poverty? To answer this question, we must look at God's nature in His word. Jesus was anointed by the Holy Spirit to *"preach the gospel to the poor"* in Luke 4:18 and in Luke 6:20 He says" ...*Blessed be ye poor: for yours is the kingdom of God.*" These two verses (among many) show God's love toward the poor of the earth. By this we can plainly see that when our title scripture states that *"the destruction of the poor is their poverty,"* that God is not the culprit. The wrongdoer is poverty. While God gives riches that construct or fortify, the devil, through poverty, brings destruction. In John 10:10 Jesus refers to the devil as "the thief." This thief *cometh not but for to steal, and to kill, and to destroy.* By poor choices, bad habits, foolishness and sin, poverty is invited into one's life and destroys. The only way out of its destructive clutches is to forsake the things that it uses to trap us. God is not glorified by poverty, especially when it is affecting the lives of believers. It is also important to note that poverty destroys not only the poor, but even the rich that make unwise choices. Poverty does not discriminate. It is an equal opportunity destroyer. The solution is found in turning to God who Psalm 103:4 says, *"redeemeth thy life from destruction."*

When poverty is around the poor are torn down

Is Life Building You Up or Tearing You Down?

STOP BEING STINGY

THERE IS THAT SCATTERETH AND YET INCREASETH; AND *THERE IS* THAT
WITHOLDETH MORE THAN IS MEET, BUT *IT TENDETH* TO POVERTY.

Proverbs 11:24

There is one that increases by not holding back

And one that withholds much and tends to lack.

The Bible tells us that…*the earth is the LORD's and the fulness thereof, the world and
all that dwell therein* (Psalms 24:1). God says in Haggai 2:8: *The silver is Mine, and the gold is
Mine saith the LORD of hosts*. How, then, can we be closefisted with what belongs to God?
The word stingy is defined as unwilling to give or spend; ungenerous.

The animated show Duck Tales featured the renowned Scrooge McDuck. In the cartoon
kingdom he was the richest of the rich, but he did not have the name Scrooge for naught. The
trillionaire, (yes, trillionaire) duck was as miserly as they come. His love for his money was
seemingly only rivaled by his love for his three grandnephews, Hewey, Dewey and Louie. The
more apparent message, however, was that if you have money you had better guard it all costs.

There are those that would argue that this passage is referring to the benefits of investing.
They say that to scatter means to diversify. It is true that the Bible does encourage investing.
However, this is not what "scatter" means here. It derives from a Hebrew word meaning "to
disperse.' It is a farming term for sowing, but it is figuratively used regarding a bountiful giver.
The apostle Paul writes*: He which soweth sparingly shall reap also sparingly; and he which
soweth bountifully shall reap also bountifully.* (2 Corinthians 9:6)

What is it then that leads to poverty? The lead passage tells us that withholding more
than is meet tends to poverty. God is not a socialist. The word tells us that one who has riches is
not obligated to become broke to appease others. The truth is that giving to those in need is to
bless them as you have been blessed by God. Withholding your resources conveys the message
that you are responsible for your own blessing. Unfortunately, it is a magnet for poverty,
because God looks out for the poor and needy and will use your resources to take care of them
even if you will not.

Holding riches back leads to lack

Are You Giving and Increasing or Withholding and Decreasing?

RICHES CAN'T BE TRUSTED

HE THAT TRUSTETH IN HIS RICHES SHALL FALL: BUT THE RIGHTEOUS SHALL FLOURISH AS A BRANCH.

Proverbs 11:28

He that trusts in his riches shall fall down

But the righteous, shall as a branch, abound

How often have we heard the statement, "If I just had enough money, then everything would be all right?" We may have heard it come from our own lips. When bills are piling up or when we need provision, then having enough money seems to be our go to response. Yet we are continually warned in Proverbs about the dangers of trusting in riches:

Wilt thou set thine eyes upon that which is not? For *riches* certainly make themselves wings, they fly away as an eagle toward heaven. (Proverbs 23:5)

For riches *are* not forever: and doth the crown *endure* to every generation? (Proverbs 27:24)

Are riches a bad thing? No. Not unless we put our trust in them instead of God who gave them. Trusting in money or anything more than God is showing distrust towards Him. If we put our trust in riches, which are unstable, then what happens when they fall? The interesting thing about Solomon's warning is that he emphasizes that *"he that trusteth in his riches shall fall.* The condemnation is not for trusting in riches, but in trusting in riches that are not *his* to begin with. God says in Haggai 2:8: *The silver is Mine and the gold is Mine, saith the LORD of hosts.*

We are on this borrowed earth, with borrowed resources, on borrowed time. Our complete trust should be in the One who lends us the resources and not the resources themselves. That is idolatry. Our focus is to be on being righteous before God whom causes us to flourish. We should wisely consider what God will be looking for in judgement. Will He be concerned about how rich we are in money or how rich we are in righteousness? Proverbs 11:4 gives us a stern warning:

Riches profit not in the day of wrath; but righteousness delivereth from death.

The equation is simple: Riches over righteousness = Death. Righteousness over Riches = Life

Riches trusted will leave you broke and busted

Are You Falling for Riches or Flourishing in Righteousness?

TROUBLING YOUR HOUSE

HE THAT TROUBLETH HIS OWN HOUSE SHALL INHERIT THE WIND; AND THE
FOOL *SHALL* BE SERVANT TO THE WISE IN HEART.

Proverbs 11:29

He that troubles his own house shall inherit the wind

To be a wise man's slave shall be the fool's end

Could you imagine working day and night to accumulate wealth by any
means necessary only to inherit… nothing? Worse still, what about doing illegal
things or engaging in unethical activities just to make a buck? Does it make sense
to trouble the very house that you are trying to bless?

Before we proceed, perhaps it would be best to define, "house" as described
in this passage, the word house has a variety of applications from the obvious,
house or home, to the extended versions meaning family, temple, ministry or
business. To bring trouble to any one of the areas of one's life is
counterproductive.

As a matter of fact, before one can properly build a house, he must have a
proper foundation. Proverbs 24:3 *tells us that through wisdom is an house
builded…* Verse 27 of the same chapter admonishes us to:

Prepare thy work without, and make it fit for thyself in the field, and afterwards
build thine house.

Borrowing a popular phrase pertaining to trouble: "Don't start none, it won't
be none." In other words, if you do not build your house with trouble, then trouble
cannot tear it down in the end. A house, family, ministry or career built on trouble
is destined to crumble. Such action is deemed as foolish. To receive bribes, cut
corners or operate in unethical means to advance one's cause is foolish and
destructive. The foolish will only inherit the wind. As for the wise in heart or
those that build a house with Godly wisdom, they shall inherit glory.

A house built on trouble is a house on the bubble.

Are You Troubling Your House or Building a Wise Legacy?

LAZY BONES

THE HAND OF THE DILIGENT SHALL BEAR RULE: BUT THE SLOTHFUL SHALL BE UNDER TRIBUTE.

Proverbs 12:24

The hand of the diligent shall rule the land,

But the slothful shall be under the debtor's hand.

Steven K. Scott, in his book, *The Richest Man Who Ever Lived,* defined diligence as more than just persistent hard work or effort. He defines true diligence as:

A learnable skill that combines creative persistence, a smart-working effort rightly planned and rightly performed in a timely, efficient and effective manner to attain a result that is pure and of the highest quality of excellence.

Sounds easy enough right? All sarcasm aside; at first glance this would appear to be a daunting task. One would be inclined to think that one would have had to be born with "diligent genes" and that this only applies to those that do. However, the truth is that diligence, like any other attribute, is a learnable skill. The Bible tells us in James 3:17 that *the wisdom from above is...easy to be intreated...* in other words, if anyone applies God's wisdom as instructed it will work for them. Reading, and more importantly, applying the word of God in our lives causes us to walk in the same authority as the word itself. Who better to rule than the one who follows the way of the Ruler of all things? The truth is that those that are diligent are trusted to lead, because they not only put the work in, but do it excellently.

This concept is not a new one. It dates back millennia. Unfortunately, so does slothfulness. It is the slothful that end up working for those that are diligent. Yet many find themselves perplexed as to why some seem to get ahead while others seem to stay stagnant. Well, perhaps slothfulness is the culprit. Slothfulness, according to Strong's Exhaustive Concordance is not merely laziness. It has more to do with treachery or deceit. There are those in our society that feel that they can manipulate the system or finagle their way through life. However, sowing deceitful seeds will reap a deceitful harvest. Take credit cards for an example. Though there is nothing illegal about credit card spending, it is deceitful to "spend" the money and not pay back what you borrowed. It is not so much about deceiving them as it is deceiving ourselves into thinking that we could easily pay it back with the high interest payment. Consequently, we remain under tribute to those who diligently suckered us in to getting the cards in the first place.

Lazy bones and payday loans bring future groans and moans.

Are You a Diligent Ruler or a Lazy Slave?

SLUG LIFE

THE SOUL OF THE SLUGGARD DESIRETH, AND *HATH* NOTHING; BUT THE SOUL OF THE DILIGENT SHALL BE MADE FAT.

Proverbs 13:4

The sluggard has nothing though his soul may plead,

But a diligent soul is made fat, indeed.

Ever seen a slug move? It is excruciatingly slow. It has been recorded to cover 6.5 inches in 120 minutes. Yawn. It takes little imagination to see how the term "sluggard" is derived from slug. A sluggard is a lazy or indolent person. Something worth noting in this scripture is that it is not the sluggard himself that desires, but the *soul* of the sluggard that desires. The soul is made up of our mind, will and emotions. The sluggard then is not a sluggard on the inside, but on the outside. God has provided him with a mind, will and emotions to desire that is held captive by the sluggard. Many suffer from the effects of a suppressed soul. There may be a desire to prosper on the inside, but the flesh will not cooperate.

3 John 2 gives us a depiction of how our soul works in conjunction with our health and prosperity. He says:

Beloved I wish above all things that thou mayest prosper and be in health,

even as thy soul prospereth.

As the soul prospers, everything else prospers. Could it be that the soul of a man has been designed by God to prosper us and allow us to walk in divine health? Could the residue of our past, our environments, and the negative effects of our hurts and disappointments be stifling our soul power?

The latter part of this passage may give us a clue: …but the soul of the diligent shall be made fat. If the soul of the sluggard desires and has nothing, then the soul of the diligent desires and is made fat. To be made fat in the Hebrew specifically means "to anoint." Whoa!

The soul is neutral. If the mind, will and emotions are subject to the flesh, then the desire is hindered. If the soul's attributes are subject to the Spirit, it is anointed by the Spirit to accomplish the desire. In the words of Proverbs 13:19:

The desire accomplished is sweet to the soul…

Sluggish souls can never achieve goals

17

Are You Slacking and Lacking or Healthy and Wealthy?

WHERED'YA GET THOSE RICHES?

THERE IS THAT MAKETH HIMSELF RICH, YET *HATH* NOTHING: *THERE* IS THAT MAKETH HIMSELF POOR, YET *HATH* GREAT RICHES.

Proverbs 13:7

There is that makes himself rich, yet has nothing to show

There is that makes himself poor, but has great riches, though

Jesus tells a parable in Luke 12: 16-21 warning about the dangers of being rich in goods, but not being rich toward God:

And He spake a parable unto them, saying the ground of a certain rich man brought forth plentifully. And he thought within himself, saying, what shall I do, because I have no more room where to bestow my fruits? And he said, this will I do: I will pull down my barns, and build greater, and there will I bestow all my fruits and my goods. But God said unto him, Thou fool, this night thy soul shall be required of thee: then whose shall those things be, which thou hast provided? So is he that layeth up treasure for himself and is not rich toward God.

The term "self-made millionaire" abounds in our society. It carries a great amount of esteem. Though it is admirable for one to work hard to attain such status, it is dangerous for one to forget that it was God who made it possible. What can man obtain that God does not allow? John the Baptist admonishes us that we ...***can receive nothing unless it is given to us from heaven*** (John 3:27). It is quite easy for man to lose sight of what is unseen. An invisible God who gives the power and ability to inhale and exhale seems ludicrous to many, much less the ability to get wealth. Just because God is not seen does not mean that He is not present. An arrogant or boastful attitude can be catastrophic. An air of superiority or lofty views of self-importance can be a long distance to fall from. It oftentimes takes one crisis to cause one to lose it all. Material possessions, goods, investments, relationships and even life should be counted as blessings and not entitlements.

But what about those that *are* "rich toward God?" Those that recognize that God not only allows wealth, but bestows it realize that they have a responsibility to help others in need as God directs. He does not call for those that have been diligent to sustain those who refuse to be. He does, however, grant those that choose to not allow their riches to put them on a pedestal, but rather causes them to walk more in humility, to delight in true riches. Greater than all the money in the world is an intimate relationship and fellowship with the One who owns it all.

Did you earn or save or was it God who gave?

Are You Rich Yet Poor or Poor Yet Rich?

VAIN MONEY

WEALTH *GOTTEN* BY VANITY SHALL BE DIMINISHED: BUT HE THAT GATHERETH
BY LABOUR SHALL INCREASE

Proverbs 13:11

Wealth gotten by vanity shall be diminished

But he that gathers by labor shall be replenished

The ways to make money in this world are as numerous as every man's imagination. The common adage is" that if you can perceive it, then you can achieve it." Quite frankly, if one is able put in the effort to bring about their ideas, success is guaranteed. But what happens if the mind that one uses to perceive and achieve is flawed? What happens when one thinks with a vain mind? After all, the Bible gives us another common saying that, "…as a man soweth, that shall he also reap," In other words, vain thoughts result in vain actions. Vain imaginations result in vain manifestations.

The Hebrew word for vanity is *hebel* (heh-bel) which is translated as "emptiness.' Therefore, this passage conveys the meaning that wealth gotten by emptiness produces emptiness. What else could it produce? An example of wealth gotten by vanity is ill gotten gain or "blood money." Countless prison sentences and deaths have been the result of these vain pursuits. It would sometimes seem that crime does in fact, pay. What it pays, however, is hardly ever worth the cost. Most assuredly, these vain pursuits are highly deceitful, because they appear to be profitable outwardly. Upon closer inspection they are valueless. Such pursuits are the quickest path to poverty.

What about the flip side? Increase that comes as a result of labor is boundless. The word tells us that it is God that gives increase. Who does He give it to? The better question would be: "What does He give it to?" God gives increase to honest work. He not only gives wealth but increasing wealth. My Dad used to tell me that 'it is not hard to make money. The challenge is to keep the money you make." What I have personally learned is that making money God's way allows you not only to keep it, but to guarantee its increase.

Vanity will cause increase to cease

Is Your Labor in Vain?

CAN'T TELL ME NUTHIN'

POVERTY AND SHAME *SHALL BE TO* HIM THAT REFUSETH INSTRUCTION: BUT HE THAT REGARDETH REPROOFSHALL BE HONOURED.

Proverbs 13:18

To him that refuses instruction comes poverty and shame

But he that regards reproof shall have an honored name

Know-it-alls are poverty magnets. Though it is true that having knowledge and expertise in a given field is crucial to financial success, the refusal to continue to learn and grow can be devastating. Several corporate giants and industry powerhouses have had to close their doors because they refused to grow and adapt to society's changing demands. As I sit here typing on this laptop, I am reminiscent of how the typewriter that I used in high school is virtually obsolete. A college friend of mine had a father who was instrumental in developing the Smith-Corona typewriter. I have yet to see the Smith-Corona laptop or computer. Years ago, we might have thought such a thing unthinkable. I wonder if some young executive was in the meeting trying to warn them that they had better look into computer technology, or they would someday cease to be relevant?

Sometimes, however, the reverse can be true. As generation leads to generation, society abounds with young ambitious know-it-alls that scoff at the wisdom of experience. The proverbial saying, "I know, but" seems to take precedence over receiving instruction. The Bible warns us that refusing instruction leads to poverty and shame. Such refusal will lead not only to being broke, but also to being broken. All because one would rather show than know. But such a façade will be exposed as fraud. Refusing instruction and correction can have devastating results. Recently, a renowned aeronautics company approved the flight of a jumbo jet for the public. Upon closer inspection, it was discovered that a crucial component necessary for flight safety was malfunctioning. Rather than ground the flights, the company neglected to warn the airlines so as not to affect profits. As a result, hundreds of people were killed in two separate flights. What's more is that the planes ended up being grounded anyway, costing the company millions. All of which could have been avoided by heeding instruction.

Thank God for those that take heed to correction. Those that are humble enough to learn from their mistakes shall be honored. Why? Because their desire is not to get by, but to get it right. As we saw in the previous tragic story, cutting corners could cost lives. Our day to day activities should be treated with the same significance. Proverbs 15:33 says that: *The fear of the Lord is the beginning of wisdom and before honor is humility.* Humility is as crucial in learning from one's mistakes as wisdom is for correcting them. It could mean the difference between poverty and wealth, shame and honor, or life and death.

Learn and turn or you will never earn

Are You Still Willing to Learn?

GIVE ME MY INHERITANCE…AND YOURS, TOO

A GOOD *MAN* LEAVETH AN INHERITANCE TO HIS CHILDREN'S CHILDREN; AND THE WEALTH OF THE SINNER *IS* LAID UP FOR THE JUST.

Proverbs 13:22

A good man leaves his grandchild a trust,

but the wealth of the sinner is laid up for the just.

Here is another one of those awesome benefits for those that desire to do good. Not only will someone that pursues goodness leave something to his children and grandchildren, but God allows them to plunder the sinner's wealth as well. Wow! A similar scripture depicting this wealth transfer is found in Ecclesiates 2:26:

For God giveth to a man that *is good* in His sight wisdom, and knowledge and joy: but to the sinner he giveth travail, to gather and to heap up, that He may give *to him that is good* before God. This also *is* vanity and vexation of spirit.

Although these passages demonstrate the advantages of being good before God, the primary objective is to show the pitfalls of poverty. For instance, we see that for a good person to receive an inheritance to leave to his future generations, the wealth must be stored up by someone for distribution. It would appear, that this responsibility falls solely on the person doing good. But if that were the case, it would contradict Proverbs 10:22 which says:

The blessing of the LORD, maketh rich and He addeth no sorrow with it.

The word *sorrow* here means "painful toil" or 'labor.' This simply means that the good person's inheritance is not based on his effort, but as a result of God's blessing. The blessing of the LORD gives one the wisdom and knowledge to enjoy that blessing. Contrarily, He let's the sinner work, hustle and strive only to have that work" transferred" to those who do good. The author of Ecclesiastes calls this "vanity and vexation of spirit," but not to the good. Rather it is the one who chooses to remain in unrepentant sin and rely on his own effort to prosper. The result is a road of misery that leads to poverty.

The sinner's cash will be the good person's stash.

Who Are You Leaving It For?

QUIT BELLY ACHIN'

THE RIGHTEOUS EATETH TO THE SATISFYING OF THE SOUL: BUT THE BELLY OF THE WICKED SHALL WANT

Proverbs 13:25

The soul is satisfied when the righteous eat

But the belly of the wicked shall lack meat

A good buffet with great food is just about heavenly. Having your pick of so many delicacies at one time is a wonder to behold. At most buffets, if you do not see the dish that you desire, then there is a chef that will make it for you, special order. This is how it is with God's righteous ones. Through Christ, we have our pick of the finest that life has to offer. Not only do we have free choice, but free access. As good as buffets are, I have never seen a free one. One might say, there is nothing free, somebody paid for this. You are correct. 2 Corinthians 5:21 says:

For He (God) hath made Him (Jesus) to be sin who knew no sin;

that we might be made the righteousness of God in Him.

The truth is that none of us is righteous by his own merit. You cannot earn that distinction. The key is to *know* that we have been made righteous, because we did not know how to be. This is awesome news because through Christ we can eat all we want until we are satisfied. Would it not be a sad sight to enter an all-you-can-eat buffet and sit down at a table waiting for them to take your order? Imagine how upset you'd get watching other people eating platefuls and no one has even bothered to hand you a menu. After several grueling minutes you finally flag down a manager to complain about not being served. The manager looks at you as though you were an alien from the Planet Dummy yet politely smiles and says "umm…this is a buffet, you can serve yourself from all that we have to offer."

All jokes aside this is sadly what is keeping believers from having all the Father has to offer. Though this passage tells us the "belly of the wicked shall want," it is worse to be a righteous person with a wicked belly. The Lord says that His "people perish for lack of knowledge." It is not because they must, but because they lack the knowledge of who they are.

Blessed are they that hunger and thirst, for they shall be filled. Now get to the buffet!

Get off your seat and go eat

What Are You Hungering and Thirsting After?

I HEAR YA TALKIN' BUT

IN ALL LABOR THERE IS PROFIT: BUT THE TALK OF THE LIPS *TENDETH* ONLY TO PENURY.

Proverbs 14:23

In all labor, there is money to fill your bags

But mere talk turns your riches into rags

In all labor there is a profit of some sort. Even negative labor will produce negative results. Physical inactivity can yield poor health, circulation or even atrophied muscles. Neglected relationships can lead to breakup or, in marriage, divorce. One might think that this is not labor, but rather the lack thereof. But doing nothing *is* labor, because it is a choice to do something and that something, is nothing. The point here is not to be facetious, but to show that there is always action taken and that action results in a reaction. Even avoidance and procrastination are actions to prolong having to act.

To produce a positive profit requires positive labor. It sounds simple, but many times we are astounded by the results we get as though our labor had nothing to do with the outcome. Sure, mistakes are bound to happen. Good intentions can result in failure. These outcomes, however, are only a message to make changes in the labor to get the result that we want from that labor. It is not that it does not work, but rather that it has not worked yet,

Keeping with the scope of this book, we must focus on the trap of poverty. With this verse specifically, we need to see how mere talk leads us to that trap. A proper illustration to describe how this process works might be to view idle talk and poverty as a road map. **If idle talk is your road map, then, according to this passage, your destination is penury or poverty.** If you travel and end up at the *wrong* destination, then you have gone the *wrong* way. If you travel and end up at the *right* destination, then you have gone the *right* way. Even if you feel that you have gone the wrong way and end up at the right destination, then you have not gone the wrong way, but rather a *different* way.

Mere talk will lead us somewhere and that somewhere is poverty. If that is not the desired destination, then the route must change. If profit, that is *good* profit, is your preferred destination, then the path of good labor is the only way to go.

Idle talk is a poverty walk

Is Your Work Speaking for Itself?

AN IDLE SOUL

SLOTHFULNESS CASTETH INTO A DEEP SLEEP; AND AN IDLE SOUL SHALL
SUFFER HUNGER

Proverbs 19:15

Slothfulness casts one into a deep sleep

On an idle soul shall hunger creep

Ever been so sleepy that you miss the alarm clock? When you finally awake you realize that you did not miss it after all, but that you turned it off without realizing? This, my friend is a deep sleep. But not so deep as the sleep that is described here. The term "deep sleep" here is from the Hebrew word *tardemah* (tar-day-maw), which translates into lethargy or trance. It is virtually hypnotic.

The point is that slothfulness is a powerful anesthesia. How powerful? So powerful that Solomon says that it *casteth* into a deep sleep. The word *casteth* is not to be viewed lightly. Some of its synonyms are: to fall, fall down, divide, overthrow. An appropriate visual might be like being in a boxing match. Slothfulness would be the undefeated champion that delivers a right hook that sends the lazy man to the canvas. Even when the defeated sloth gets up, he still is dazed and confused.

What about the idle soul? The Word says that they shall suffer hunger. The truth is that all of us get hungry. Even Jesus got hungry. Our bodies are designed to alert us when they need food. There is a difference though, in being hungry and suffering hunger. Being hungry is usually temporary, but to *suffer* hunger is a continual state that implies that one does not know where his next meal is coming from. Truly, there are those that live in adverse conditions where hunger is beyond their control. This verse here, however, is talking about one that is hungry, but refuses to forsake his laziness to feed himself. He suffers, but unnecessarily, but he suffers, nonetheless.

Street corners are riddled with people that have fallen on hard times. There are few places that one can go where a person is asking for money to buy food. Granted that there are panhandlers among the group, that have homes while pretending to be homeless. Many have equipped themselves with the art of storytelling to provoke empathy. Though their intentions may not be clear to passersby, their motives are completely clear to God. It would seem, that they are somehow immune to this scripture, but not so. Despite their motives this verse is not about moral ramifications as it is about cause and effect. They may appear idle because they do not conform to society's norms, but they are not idle in their determination to beg. Regardless of their methods, it fills their bellies. The sad part is that slothfulness has them in a "trance" that keeps them in poverty and their souls in hunger.

Slothfulness keeps you in bed and idleness keeps you unfed

Are You Working Toward What You Are Hungry For?

HURRY, HURRY!

THE THOUGHTS OF THE DILIGENT *TEND* ONLY TO PLENTEOUSNESS; BUT OF EVERYONE *THAT IS* HASTY ONLY TO WANT.

Proverbs 21:5

The thoughts of the diligent always abound

But the hasty will look and only lack will be found

The thoughts of the diligent always lead to prosperity. That is because the diligent do not just think about what they will do, they act until their thoughts lead to success. The word diligence is a mining term. Solomon used many mining terms in his proverbs, because he had great success in his ventures mining for precious metals and stones. He derived experience in these areas and translated it to other areas in his life.

The word *diligent* is from the Hebrew word *charuts* (khaw-roots') which is synonymous with a 'dug trench" or "mined gold." Notice that these definitions are past tense. A trench that is already dug and gold that is already mined. These tenses show how important the word diligent is. Unlike passive thinking, diligent thoughts begin in the past tense. In other words, when the diligent think of something, it, to them, is already done. Not only is it already done, but it is already plenteous. After all, is not gold, already gold before it is mined?

What about the flip side of diligence, hastiness? Diligence is to plenteousness as hastiness is to poverty. Poverty loves hastiness, because hastiness is a byproduct of ignorance. The diligent pursue only what they know is valuable or worthwhile. The hasty pursue whatever they can get their hands on, with hopes that it may be valuable. Hastiness is a gamble with impossible odds. The only prize in this pursuit of poverty.

We should keep in mind the greatest treasures in life are things that money cannot buy.

Philippians 4:8 Finally, brethren whatsoever things *are* true, whatsoever things *are* honest, whatsoever things *are* just, whatsoever things *are* pure, whatsoever things *are* lovely, whatsoever things *are* of a good report, *if there be* any virtue, and *if there be* any praise, think on these things.

The lesson learned here is that diligent thoughts trump hasty actions any day.

The diligent succeed while the hasty need

Is Your Work Gaining or Draining?

YOU SNOOZE, YOU LOSE

LOVE NOT SLEEP LEST THOU COME TO POVERTY; OPEN THINE EYES, *AND* THOU SHALT BE SATISFIED WITH BREAD.

Proverbs 20:13

Love not to sleep lest thou come to lack

Open eyes shall give you bread in your sack

Imagine a person rising day by day before the sun rises. Your weekly routine demands that you rise early and get to bed late. Now, envision your weekend or holiday when you get to sleep. There is no need for the alarm clock, because this is your time to sleep in. There is nothing wrong with that. The word of God supports sleep:

It is vain for you to rise up early, to sit up late, to eat the bread of sorrows:

For so He giveth His beloved sleep. (Psalm 127:2)

Scripture also says:

When thou liest down, thou shalt not be afraid: yea, thou shalt lie down,

and thy sleep shall be sweet. (Proverbs 3:24)

Sleep, then, is not the culprit. It is even accepted and granted by God. How then can something given by God, Who gives blessing, lead to poverty? The problem does not lie in sleep, but in the *love* of sleep. The usage of the word "love" in this passage is the Hebrew word *aheb* which means to "have affection for." How does this lead to poverty? This could be better understood by another familiar passage in the Apostle Paul's letter to Timothy. In 1 Timothy 6:10 he warns:

For the **love** of money is the root of all evil: which while some coveted after, they have erred from the faith, and pierce themselves through with many sorrows.

It is a common misconception (and commonly corrected) that money itself is the root of all evil. The scripture, however, warns that it is the *love* of money that is the root cause. Sleep, like money, is inherently neutral. The danger lies in misplaced affection. One's affection for something that is not designed by God to garner that affection is idolatrous. Anything *loved* is served. When anything that was created to serve us, becomes what we serve, it cannot prosper. It will certainly lead to poverty. Sleep, like all things supplied by God, should be moderate. Excessiveness cannot only be detrimental to our health, but also hazardous to our wealth,

Poverty will creep on those who love sleep

35

Which Is Better: Awoke or Broke?

PLEASURE, OIL, & WINE, ERADICATES RICHES

HE THAT LOVETH PLEASURE *SHALL BE* A POOR MAN: HE THAT LOVETH OIL AND WINE
SHALL NOT BE RICH Proverbs 21:17

A poor man shall a lover of pleasure be.

From him that loves wine and oil, shall riches flee

Pleasure, oil and wine in moderation are harmless. As stated previously, however, excessiveness in anything can be detrimental to your health and hazardous to your wealth. It is not merely pleasure that leads to being poor, but the *love* of pleasure. It is not the possession of oil and wine that keeps one from being rich, but the affection towards both that leads down that path. Pleasure, as discussed here, is mirth or glee. It is, when properly sought, an admirable pursuit. When God is the Source of that pleasure it is most satisfying. Job 36:11 says:

If they obey and serve *Him*, they shall spend their days in prosperity, and their years in pleasures.

So, pleasure is given by God for our enjoyment. But since it is something given by God it is not be used in a way that will dishonor Him. Pleasure found in sin is a misuse of the gift of God. **Pleasure's focus should not be more about *feeling* good than *being* good.** In various cultures around the world there are feasts, festivals, celebrations and parties of all kinds. Even the Bible speaks of God's commandment to Israel to celebrate feasts to commemorate history.

Jesus' first recorded miracle was at a wedding feast in Cana. This is worth noting because the miracle that He performed at the feast was changing water into wine. At such feasts it was socially devastating for the host of that party to run out of wine for his guests. A religious mind might take issue with this. Such might think that Jesus would refuse such a request and even rebuke them for desiring more wine. But Jesus' concern (as always) was to glorify the Father. Changing the water into wine was not so much an endorsement for wine as for God's love. It was no more an endorsement for drunkenness as it was when Jesus used it to commemorate His shed blood at Calvary during the *Last Supper*. **Loving the wine is not the object, but loving the Lord is.**

The word for oil here is the same as the oil used throughout the Old Testament. Oil is symbolic in the Bible for the anointing. This use was ordained by God. Oil was used by prophets to anoint kings. Oil was used in religious ceremonies. Oil was even used in cooking. The prophet Elisha imparted a blessing upon a widow who was due to lose her two sons to slavery to pay off a debt. Elisha instructed her to have her sons gather jars from all over in which she poured oil from one cruse. God multiplied the oil so much that when she sold it, she had enough to pay off the outstanding debt, and was able to live comfortably off the profits. What God multiplies is for His glory. Man's attempts to do this for himself or by himself lead to poverty.

Too much oil, wine, and pleasure will zap your treasure

Which Is Better: Pleasure or Treasure?

EDWARD LAZY HANDS

THE DESIRE OF THE SLOTHFUL KILLETH HIM; FOR HIS HANDS REFUSE TO LABOR

Proverbs 21:25

Around the desire of the wicked, death does lurk

For his hands refuse to do any work

Desire, as given by God, is good. When kept in its proper perspective it can be a positive motivator. It is defined as a strong feeling of wanting to have something or wishing for something to happen. Scripture supports this in various verses. In Psalm 37:4 the bible tells us:

Delight thyself also in the LORD; and He shall give thee the desires of thine heart.

In the New Testament Jesus tells us in Mark 11:24:

Therefore, I say unto you, what things soever ye desire, when ye pray, believe that ye receive *them* and ye shall have *them.*

These two verses alone clearly support that God gave man desire and that properly used it is crucial in receiving the blessings of God. When our desire aligns with God's will it most assuredly manifests. What the Lord puts in our heart will be put in our hands when desire is directed in a way that pleases Him.

But what about when desire is improperly implemented? It can become a perilous pursuit. Desire for money can become greed which can lead to robbery or burglary. Desire for pleasure can become lust which can lead to adultery. Desire for what belongs to others can become covetousness which can lead to idolatry. So, the desire to avoid diligence can become slothfulness which can lead to death. How? Proverbs 13:12 sheds some light on the subject:

Hope deferred maketh the heart sick, but when the desire cometh it is a tree of life.

What we see then is that deferred desire can give us spiritual heart disease. It brings spiritual and even physical death. True desire can only come when it is brought about as God intended. The truth is that the desire of the slothful is to, well, be slothful. It is that desire, that if left unchanged, can be disastrous.

Slothful desire can prove to be dire

Are You Desiring What Your Labor Deserves?

REVERSE ROBIN HOOD

HE THAT OPPRESSETH THE POOR TO INCREASE HIS *RICHES*, *AND* HE THAT GIVETH TO THE RICH, *SHALL* SURELY *COME* TO WANT.

Proverbs 22:16

He that oppresses the poor to fill his money sack

And gives to the rich, shall surely lack.

Excluding more recent generations, most have heard the tales of the legendary Robin Hood. The hero who robbed the rich tyrannical powers that be to give to the poor and the downtrodden. The concept, although valiant, was still criminal. This might make for exciting storytelling, but it presents a message that taking matters into one's own hands is the way to go, even if it is a lesser evil. As the saying goes" two wrongs don't make a right."

Unlike the tales of Robin Hood, however, the focus of this passage is on the oppression of the poor by the rich. Oppressing the rich is no more morally sound than oppressing the poor. The key word here is oppresseth. It is defined in the Hebrew language as to defraud, violate, or wrong. A more unusual definition means to overflow or drink up. Whatever the definition of choice, all roads lead to destruction. More likely, it is the rich that have the power and resources to institute the oppression. The primary purpose of that oppression being to increase their riches. Biblical history tells us how the Israelites were oppressed by Pharaoh for four hundred years to increase the wealth and might of Egypt. There was, however. a day of reckoning when God stripped them bare through mighty plagues. God caused them to give up all their precious treasure for fear of the Israelites. Thus, the oppressors became the oppressed and the rich became poor.

The title verse also expresses a warning to those that give to the rich. The word giveth means what it says. But giving *to* the rich *by* the rich is just as offensive as oppressing the poor. The reason is because it kept available resources from getting to the poor and needy. Some oppressed the poor while others neglected them, but a day always comes when God levels the playing field. In the New Testament James warns the rich oppressors of their upcoming judgment: *Go to now, ye rich men, weep and howl for your miseries that shall come upon you. (James5:1)*

Heaven may have streets that are made with gold, but the streets of greed all lead to poverty.

When rich oppressors trade gifts their prosperity drifts.

Are You Oppressing Others or Blessing Others?

COSIGN BLUES

BE NOT THOU *ONE* OF THEM THAT STRIKE HANDS, *OR* OF THEM THAT ARE
SUERTIES FOR DEBTS. IF THOU HAST NOTHING TO PAY, WHY SHOULD HE TAKE
AWAY THY BED FROM UNDER THEE?

Proverbs 22:26-27

Don't be one that strikes hand to hand or be a bookie's debtor man

Because if you don't have the money to pay, then why should he take your bed away?

Debt is serious business. Currently the United States of America has a whopping $16 trillion dollars in debt. Wow! It seems to support the illusion that being in debt is no big deal. It is a sign that debt is the accepted norm. If the nation's leaders are advocating this by continually spending while being in debt, then what is the message to the citizens?

The above scripture warns against the danger of loans. The term "strike hands" at first glance might appear to mean to fight someone. The words in this verse though, mean to shake hands to make a bond with someone. It is common in many cultures to shake hands to agree on a business deal or promise. In this proverb Solomon is not condemning such agreement so much as he is speaking against doing so when you have no money to back up the agreement. This warning is not only for one's own debt, but also for the sake of others. If we do not have the money, then it is best not to get into debt. Even worse is promising to pay a debt for some else, when neither one of you have the money. Cosigning is never a good idea.

Our societies make it so easy to get into such agreements, but difficult to get out. Does that not sound a lot like how a trap works? Now let us imagine a friend or loved one that is about to enter that same trap but cannot. Is it then wise to help them to enter that trap? Won't we both end up trapped? If we are both blindly leading each other, then are we not both likely to fall into the same pit? This is the danger of cosigning for another's debt. Having personally been on both sides of this same coin was harmful and embarrassing. It has caused strained relationships, lost property, repossession and damaged credit.

Patience is a virtue. It is better to patiently wait until we have the money for what we are purchasing than rushing into debt. This especially applies if securing that debt requires dragging someone else's good name (or credit) into the debt as well. There have been countless instances where furniture, cars, homes and the like have been taken, for failure to honor debts. The truth is that there is nothing honorable about this system and it is best to avoid it if possible. Regarding this trap it is best to take the advice of one rat to the other rat when he said., "whatever you do, do not take the cheese."

If neither can pay, then stay away

Are You Shaking Hands with Debt?

EAT, DRINK, SLEEP, AND BE BROKE

BE NOT AMONG WINEBIBBERS; AMONG RIOTOUS EATERS OF FLESH. FOR THE DRUNKARD AND THE GLUTTON SHALL COME TO POVERTY: AND DROWSINESS SHALL CLOTHE *A MAN* WITH RAGS.

Proverbs 23:20-21

Be not among those that drink too much wine and have made gluttony their favorite pastime

For the glutton and the drunkard shall come to lack and a drowsy man shall have ragged clothes on his back

Excess can at times detract from success, because excess can distort the use of a thing. Wine in moderation is not as harmful as wine in excess. In other words, wine for a drink is okay, but wine for a drunk can have dire consequences. When a social drinker becomes a social drunk, then it can be devastating. Drunkenness has wrecked cars, wrecked homes and wrecked lives. Alcoholism has reached epidemic proportions in many cultures and is has existed as long as there was alcohol to drink.

As is for alcohol it is for food. Overeating is an epidemic in not all cultures, but many. Though there are areas on our planet where people lack the pleasure of even a decent meal to survive, there are areas where the overindulgence and waste of said food is rampant. However, this verse is not talking about merely overeating or having that extra piece of pie after dinner, but the sinful practice of gluttony. Gluttony, as defined in this verse, is not so much on the food, but on the riotous lifestyle which it entails. Such a lifestyle is sinful in its nature and drunkenness and gluttony are byproducts of that life. As the saying goes: "good company corrupts good manners." These verses warn that keeping company with drunkards and gluttons will lead to poverty.

The following verse adds a warning about the effects of drowsiness. Drowsiness is sleepiness. It is simply excessive sleep. Like a glass of wine or a satisfying meal, a peaceful sleep or power nap is acceptable. But a habit of overindulgent sleep can be hazardous to your wealth. The reason that these excessive habits are linked together in this passage is because this is usually how these events occur in life. Think about it. Wild parties and living usually lead to excessive drinking, eating and afterward a drowsy, hungover stupor. How could anyone possibly sustain a lifestyle like that? Not many. Even the rich that live in such debauchery, will ultimately crash and burns in the flames of poverty.

Riotous living drains money bags and clothes with rags

Are You Crashing with Prosperity Crashers?

FROM THE GREEDY TO THE NEEDY

HE THAT BY USURY AND UNJUST GAIN INCREASETH HIS SUBSTANCE, HE SHALL GATHER IT FOR HIM THAT WILL PITY THE POOR.

He that increases his substance by usury and unjust gain

He shall gather it for him whose pity for the poor is made plain

Wow! What an awesome promise. How many of us have been or are still in the grip of exorbitant interest payments? While it is true that many have willingly signed agreements to borrow money and pay it back, few of us are aware of the dangers of interest that keeps us from doing so. Oh, but they know that, and they hope that we do not. Month after month we send in payments with hopes that one day our loans or debts will be paid off. What many do not realize is that the bulk of those payments go to pay off interest first and not the principal; making it virtually impossible to pay off those debts. What then are we to do?

Well, this is not a book about debt consolidation or even debt elimination. There are many well qualified experts with numerous materials on that subject. The purpose here is to show the pitfalls of poverty. This pitfall is not directed just to the poor, but also to the rich. The rich and greedy companies that are making their wealth off the unsuspecting borrowers have themselves missed an important loophole. Many of these loan and credit companies are targeting the poor for their business. Sure, outwardly it looks as though they are lending you a helping hand, but the other hand is secretly taking your wallet. It may seem like a great idea to "rent-to-own" a new appliance in the beginning, but closer inspection shows its deception. For example, if a new refrigerator is $400 if you buy it directly, certain companies will allow you to pay the cost of the fridge over time at only $20 a month over 5 years. What a blessing! Great deal, right? Wrong. The same $400 appliance with interest could end up costing you in the thousands. What is worse is that if you miss one payment, then they can come a take the refrigerator no matter how many payments that are made thus far. What a tragedy.

So, what does God think about this? This passage shows that He is not pleased with such practices. A time of judgement is most certainly coming for such dealers of deceit. Their inventory is going to end up in the hands of those that will deal rightly with the poor. Our responsibility is to begin treating the poor and needy with respect and dignity. The Lord is looking for such people to give these businesses to. Jesus says that doing this in secret shall be rewarded openly. We are not to boast about how many poor people we are helping. God knows and He rewards those with blessing. Those that are making money off the backs of the poor will be rewarded with poverty. What shall be your reward?

Usury and unjust gain is a money drain

Is Being Greedy Keeping You Needy?

LEAD NOT INTO TEMPTATION

WHOSO CAUSETH THE RIGHTEOUS TO GO ASTRAY IN AN EVIL WAY, HE SHALL FALL HIMSELF INTO HIS OWN PIT: BUT THE UPRIGHT SHALL HAVE GOOD *THINGS* IN POSSESSION.

Proverbs 28:10

He will fall into a pit who leads the upright astray

But good is inherited by those that don't go that way

History is riddled with nefarious leaders leading people down wayward paths. Many unsuspecting folks have blindly followed leaders with hopes of a better life. Countless stories of cult leaders claiming to be the savior of the world have duped many with false hope. Oh, how often has this blind allegiance led to devastation and death. An outside observer might marvel at the naivete of such simpletons. No red-blooded human being with any amount of common sense should fall for such nonsense. Right?

Well, before we judge prematurely, we must realize that we have been designed to hope. God created mankind to hope and that hope is to be in...***Jesus Christ which is our hope***. (1 Timothy 1:1). Unfortunately, our hope is not always properly placed. Sometimes, we satiate that appetite for hope with unsuitable things that can be hazardous to our health and our wealth. Even the righteous can be led astray by ignorance. But woe to the one that leads them away. The word tells that he that does that ***shall fall into his own pit.*** Proverbs 26:27 also warns that:

Whoso diggeth a pit shall fall therein: and he that rolleth a stone, it will return on him.

What does this have to do with poverty? Unbeknownst to those who deceitfully swindle others, God will sometimes allow the righteous to fall in their trap. Why? So that He will have cause to bring judgment. God allowed righteous Daniel to be unjustly thrown into the den of lions. God sent an angel to stop the mouths of the lions and the same men that conspired against Daniel (along with their families) were thrown into the same pit and devoured by the same lions. Scripture further tells us that Daniel was exonerated in Daniel 6:28:

So this Daniel prospered in the reign of Darius, and in the reign of Cyrus the Persian.

As a righteous man of God Daniel was not only delivered from the pit of poverty but received a good possession for his uprightness.

He who leads the righteous astray will be poverty's prey

Whose Lead Are You Following?

SIN: THE BLESSING BLOCKER

HE THAT COVERETH HIS SINS SHALL NOT PROSPER: BUT WHOSO CONFESSETH
AND FORSAKETH *THEM* SHALL HAVE MERCY.

Proverbs 28:13

He that covers his sin shall not prosper at all

He who confesses and forsakes them, on him, mercy shall fall

In the world's system nothing is a juicy as a coverup. If it is not scandalous or rumor worthy, then it is not news worthy. Scandals have handles and sin is in. It may be good for ratings, but to the one that suffers exposure it is misery. Sin, by itself, is bad. As bad as it is, however, covered up sin is worse. Our human nature leads us to believe that the best way to deal with sin is to hide it. Numbers 32:23 says *... your sin will find you out.* In other words, your sin will catch up to you.

This is more than an idiomatic expression such as, "that was a piece of cake," or "it's in the bag." This is the infallible word of God. Its guarantee lies in the meaning of the word *covereth* which is Hebrew for conceal or hide. No surprise there. But what does the Bible say about sin that is hidden? In Psalms 69:5 David says:

O God, Thou knowest my foolishness;

And my sins are not hid from Thee.

The word sin in the title scripture, though, is more serious. Sin here means "revolt." Revolt is defined as an attempt to put an end to the authority of a person or body by rebelling. Interesting. Why does one seek to cover a rebellion? Perhaps it is because covering rebellion seems to offer the promise that there is a bigger benefit to hiding the rebellion than exposing it. Imagine that someone organized a coup to overthrow a king and offered the conspirators the reward of prestige, riches or power. But *rebellion is as the sin of witchcraft.* (1 Sam. 15:23) Now, let's say that the ruler was fully aware of their rebellion. He would most certainly ruin their secret plot. Not only would it *not* prosper, it could result in death to all conspirators. Now let's change scenarios. Provided that there was still a coup, let's imagine that rather than join the rebellion, the would-be conspirators warned the king. As a result, they are given mercy by the king and even rewarded with the same things that the rebels offered. The point is that covered sin or rebellion may be hidden from others, but never from God, because all things are... *laid bare before the eyes of Him to whom we must give account* (Hebrews 4:13 NIV).

Covered up sin is prosperity's end

Is Hidden Sin Doing You In?

DISCIPLES OF VANITY

HE THAT TILLETH HIS LAND SHALL HAVE PLENTY OF BREAD: BUT HE THAT FOLLOWETH AFTER VAIN *PERSONS* SHALL HAVE POVERTY ENOUGH.

Proverbs 28:19

He that tills his land shall have plenty of bread

He that follows vain persons shall have poverty instead.

Newsflash: farmers who work their land will have lots of food. Not surprising. Diligent farming in the right conditions will yield food: Ecclesiastes 5:9 tells us:

Moreover the profit of the earth is for all: the king *himself* is served by the field.

The truth is that in any endeavor consistent diligent work will produce a subsequent return. Proverbs 14:23 states that *in all labour there is profit...* Working is the most direct way to provide food for one's household. It is not always easy but is usually effective.

Our emphasis here is not about how the bread comes, but rather how the poverty comes. Not only how it comes, but about how it comes in abundance. Now there's a paradox. Abundant poverty. Who would want to be rich in poverty? Regardless of what one wants, poverty is drawn to vanity. What is worse is those who follow vanity will have their fill of lack. Another paradox. The word "followeth" here in the Hebrew means to" run after with hostile intent," "pursue," or "chase." In other words, it means to hunt for something. In and of itself, this is an admirable pursuit, but not when it is after "vain *persons*." Vain persons are worthless or empty things. It also refers to being in company with those that are also after worthless things. The Bible says that these people *shall have poverty enough*. This passage shows both a comparison and a contrast simultaneously. For just as he that diligently tills his land does so that he can have plenty of food, he that chases after worthless things shall have plenty of poverty. Both are diligent pursuits, but both have entirely different outcomes.

The hidden truth is that one will find what one will truly looking for. If the goal is to get abundant riches it is found by diligently working in one's field. Whether it is by working hard or working smart, it still takes work. If the goal is to get something out without putting something in, then whatever is put in will be received. Following vanity will lead to an abundance of poverty.

Following vanity to get more leads to poverty galore

Are You Truly Working in Your Field?

HASTE NOT, WANT NOT

A FAITHFUL MAN SHALL ABOUND WITH BLESSINGS; BUT HE THAT MAKETH
HASTE TO BE RICH SHALL NOT BE INNOCENT.

Proverbs 28:20

A faithful man shall with blessings abound

But he that is hasty to be rich shall bring his innocence down

To be joyful simply means to be full of joy. To be wonderful is to be full of wonder. However, the word faithful is defined today as being loyal, constant or steadfast. We have deviated from its archaic meaning which is: full of faith. On the surface, this may seem trivial, but taking a deeper look will show otherwise.

This passage of scripture leads with an important revelation about what a faithful person can expect. Solomon says that a faithful man abounds with blessings. However, this passage has been met with skepticism. There are many that have been devoutly loyal in their church, on their jobs or in their marriage and parental duties, that hardly perceive themselves as blessed. Quite the contrary. Many believe that their blood, sweat and tears have been greatly overlooked and underappreciated. If anything, they feel dejected and taken advantage of, much less blessed. Still, many suffer and endure so as not to appear ungrateful. But who are we fooling? Other people might be duped by our "I'm just gonna press on" attitude, but we cannot fool God. After all, it is He who blesses us. So, what gives?

Let us return to the old definition of faithful which is to be full of faith. If the first part of the preceding passage were read with this definition inserted, it would read: A full of faith man shall abound with blessings... See the difference? Being faithful as we are accustomed to using it keeps us drudging along believing that one day God is going to see and bless us to get out of our messes. The truth is that is not how the process works. How many people face life with the same mundane outlook everyday expecting a change, but never seeing one? Ever learning, but never turning. Always preaching, but never practicing. No change can come because we may be loyal, constant and steadfast, but to the wrong things. We loyally complain, constantly doubt and steadfastly worry, but never take time to "fill up" on our faith. Also, to *abound* is to fill up and overflow. When a glass is filled with water non-stop, then it eventually overflows. It works the same way when we "fill up" our faith. Eventually, it overflows with blessing. Being hasty, however, has the opposite effect. There is no shortcut to the blessing of the LORD. Everything done in faith will overflow with blessing. Everything done in haste repels blessing.

Haste brings waste

55

Is Your Work Faithful or Fateful?

THE EYES OF POVERTY

HE THAT HASTETH TO BE RICH HATH AN EVIL EYE,

AND CONSIDERETH NOT THAT POVERTY SHALL COME UPON HIM

Proverbs 28:22

He that makes haste to be rich, has an evil eye

And does not consider that, on him, poverty draws nigh

Being hasty to get rich is caused by blurred vision. If hastiness is the disease, then an "evil eye" is the root cause. The word "hasteth" means "to tremble inwardly," It represents a frantic state. Usually in the King James Version of the Bible, the suffix -eth denotes that the word it follows is a continued practice. Whereas *haste* alone would mean "to tremble inwardly," the word *hasteth* means to tremble inwardly continually or as a practice. What would cause someone to be in such a continual frantic state? According to this passage, it would be an "evil eye." It is no surprise that the word "evil" means bad. The analogy of the word "eye" however, is a little more intriguing. It is analogous to "a fountain." A fountain signifies a source from which something flows. In this case an eye is neutral, but what that eye is, is a choice. An eye can be bountiful as easily as it can be evil. The difference is that an evil eye leads to poverty whereas a bountiful eye is blessed. Proverbs 22:9 says that: *"He that hath a bountiful eye shall be blessed…"* Haste is a symptom of the evil eye. The evil eye stems from covetousness and envy. When one covets or is envious of another's wealth there is a danger of developing an evil eye. Jesus warns about the evil eye in Matthew 6:23: *But if thine eye be evil; thy whole body shall be full of darkness…* An evil eye is the same as an evil outlook. Everything that is viewed through the lens of the evil eye is deceptive. Instead of being able to pursue blessings with peace, it causes one to frantically chase after riches or anything that appears to be a blessing. Unfortunately, that pursuit is usually deceptive and causes stress, depression, vexation. Even worse, such a path does not only lead a man to poverty, it causes it to "come upon him" The hidden message here is that an evil eye or outlook can make one chase after riches while poverty is chasing him.

There is a term in baseball called the "good eye." According to Sportingcharts.com, having the good eye is "used in situations where extraordinary vision helps the team, such as when a pitcher spots a player at first leading too far off the bag and throws them out," Our best choice then is to develop a "good eye" towards God's goodness and receive it in return.

An evil eye draws poverty nigh

What Do You Have Your Eye On?

POOR? WHAT POOR?

HE THAT GIVETH UNTO THE POOR SHALL NOT LACK: BUT HE THAT HIDETH HIS EYES SHALL HAVE MANY A CURSE.

Proverbs 28:27

He that gives unto the poor shall not lack

But he that hides his eyes shall have many a curse brought back

Give to every man that asketh of thee; and of him that taketh away thy goods ask them not again.

Oh yes. Jesus did say that. But every man, Lord? What a bold, and yet seemingly impossible statement. But as believers always find, Jesus says what He means and means what He says. We must remember that the Lord never commanded us to do things that He did not practice Himself, nor be unable to accomplish. Granted, we may not be able to accomplish them without His assistance, but that is what He desires anyway. The word of God is consistent in its charge that rightly giving is always rewarded.

Jesus tells us in John 12:8 that:

For the poor always ye have with you; but Me ye have not always

Until Jesus returns there will always be poor people. Jesus cared for the poor and when He ascended into heaven, then it became our mission to care for them. While no one can, by himself, care for all the poor. He can care for some. Mother Theresa once said," if you cannot feed a million people, then feed one." The idea here is that there is always someone, somewhere that we can help. When Jesus tells us to give to every man that asks, it is implied that we will have something to give to them when they ask. This leads us back to our title scripture which says that he who gives t the poor shall not lack. Why not? Because God will make sure that they are always supplied in order to be able to supply others. Even if it invokes the miraculous. When Peter and John were asked by the crippled beggar at the Beautiful gate for alms, they did not have any money. Instead they gave him something much greater than money could buy. Though they had neither silver nor gold they prayed and the man who had never walked was miraculously healed. No amount of money could have bought the happiness that he received that day. God supplied Peter and John with what they needed to give the poor beggar more than what he asked for. But what would have happened if they would have "hidden their eyes" from him. He would have still been a lame beggar and the name of Jesus would not have been glorified. Not only that, but that would have cursed their pipeline from heaven. The lesson here is that God uses our eyes to watch over the poor and uses our hands to supply them.

Hiding your purse from the poor brings a curse for sure

Are You Seeing What God is Seeing?

LOOSE WOMEN, LOST MONEY

WHOSO LOVETH WISDOM REJOICETH HIS FATHER: BUT HE THAT KEEPETH COMPANY WITH HARLOTS SPENDETH *HIS* SUBSTANCE.

Proverbs 29:3

Whoever loves wisdom, his father adores

But he spends his substance that keeps company with whores

From strip malls to strip clubs there are numerous ways to be separated one from one's money. The key word here is *strip*. Both are set up to strip you of your wealth. Regardless of how much wealth one amasses, a life of riotous living can drain it dry.

Jesus tells a parable of a prodigal son who approaches his father and asks for his inheritance. Unwilling to wait until his father dies, he demands it early. This was his initial mistake. Instead of wisely "rejoicing" his father, which is a Hebraic term meaning "to make glad" he focuses on his own selfish lusts. The father complies and gives his son the inheritance which, upon receiving, packs up and heads to a "far country." Not only did he want to get far away from his father's presence, but he spent that inheritance or "substance" on "riotous living." The word "riotous" is this parable is Greek for dissolute. Some synonyms for dissolute are lewd, lustful, impure, immoral, etc. It would be safe to say that the prodigal son's excursions included harlots.

Although the parable goes on to say that he returned to his father's house who welcomed him with open arms, his company with those of ill repute zapped all his wealth and he was left all alone. It was not until he returned to rejoice his father that he was restored.

It is also important to note that this not only pertains to the wayward son, but also to the harlot. A wayward woman seeking to gain advantage from the resources of a wayward man will never satisfy. It is a miserable life to be a "gold-digger" only to find out in the end that it was only "fool's gold." In the end no one benefits from folly. If a wise son is keeping company with foolish harlots, then what does that make him? In the words of a familiar proverb: A fool and his money are soon parted.

Those of ill-repute will still your loot

Are Loose Morals Making You Lose Money?

VISION: CHERISH OR PERISH

WHERE *THERE* IS NO VISION THE PEOPLE PERISH: BUT HE THAT KEEPETH THE
LAW, HAPPY IS HE.

Proverbs 29:18

Where there is no vision, the people cast off restraint

But he that keeps the law is a happy saint

One of the main hinderances to prosperity is the lack of vision. No vision means that one cannot see where he is going. Even if he did get somewhere, he might not know if that somewhere is the place that he was supposed to be. For it is the vision that tells us where to go, how to get there and how we will know that we are there when we have arrived. After all, having no vision is doomed to fail because *starting* with no vision *ends* with no destination.

Vision in this scripture is defined as mental sight, a dream, revelation or oracle. The truth is that every road leads somewhere, even it is a dead end. Therefore, embarking on a journey that lacks vision leads to a destination that lacks prosperity. Vision is the proverbial "X" that marks the spot. Not having a map does not mean that there is no treasure, it just means that one lacks the knowledge of how to get that treasure or that it even exists. A vision given by God is a map to our destiny that comes in the form of mental sight, a dream, a revelation or oracle.

In this passage we are shown that aligning with God's vision is what leads to a happy destination. We are encouraged to keep the law. The word "keepeth" is the Hebrew word *shamar* which means hedge about, guard or attend to. The word "happy" in this verse means blessed. What we see then is that by keeping the law or the Word of God is a one-way passage to the blessings of God. The vision of God and His word are one in the same. Attempting to get the blessing of God without following the vision or word of God is futile. All such efforts and those making these efforts will "perish."

In staying consistent with our poverty trap theme, it would best to define the term "perish." The word here means to loosen or to expose. The figurative use is a bit more intriguing which means "to begin." What that says is sobering because it shows that not only will no vision lead to perishing, it prevents us from ever leaving the starting blocks. In other words, until we adopt God's way as our exclusive vision, we can never even *start* the life that He created us to live, keeping us in a perpetual state of poverty. God forbid.

No vision always leads back to lack

Do You See What God Sees?

Hebrew Translations of Poor/Poverty

Rush	In want of necessities of life	6:11; 10:4,15; 13:7.8,18,23; 14:20; 17:5; 18:23; 19:1,7,22; 22:2,7; 24:34; 28:3,6,19,27; 29:13; 30:8; 31:7
Dal	Impoverished; reduced to poverty	10:15; 14:31; 19:4,17; 22:9,16,22; 28:3,8,11,15; 29:7,14
Heser	To be in want	11:24; 21:17; 28:22
Aniy	wretched	14:21
Ebyon	Destitute; helpless	14:31
Yarash	Dispossessed	20:13; 23:21

Thank you so very much for sowing into this work and your future.

The LORD bless thee, and keep thee:

The LORD make His face shine upon thee, and be gracious unto thee:

The LORD lift up His countenance upon thee, and give thee peace.

Numbers 6:24-26

www.ingramcontent.com/pod-product-compliance
Lightning Source LLC
Chambersburg PA
CBHW030730180526
45157CB00008BA/3115

* 9 7 8 1 0 9 6 1 1 8 9 9 2 *